IF FOUND, PLEASE KINDLY RETURN TO:

NAME: _____

CELL: _____

The Mission Journal

JOURNALIST BASICS

NAME:
_____

CITY, STATE/REGION, COUNTRY OF RESIDENCE
_____
_____
_____

CITIES & COUNTRIES YOU WILL VISIT
_____
_____
_____

DATE OF TRIP: _____

THROUGH: _____

Published by David Iskander
Los Angeles, California

10 9 8 7 6 5 4 3 2 1

ISBN-13: 978-1723539800
ISBN-10: 1723539805

Copyright © David Iskander 2018

Unless otherwise indicated, all Scripture quotations are from the ESV® Bible (The Holy Bible, English Standard Version®), copyright © 2001 by Crossway, a publishing ministry of Good News Publishers. Used by permission. All rights reserved.

Scripture quotations marked (NIV) are taken from the THE HOLY BIBLE, NEW INTERNATIONAL VERSION®, NIV® Copyright © 1973, 1978, 1984, 2011 by Biblica, Inc.™ Used by permission. All rights reserved worldwide.

Scripture quotations marked MSG are taken from THE MESSAGE, copyright © 1993, 1994, 1995, 1996, 2000, 2001, 2002 by Eugene H. Peterson. Used by permission of NavPress. All rights reserved. Represented by Tyndale House Publishers, Inc.

Scripture taken from the New King James Version®. Copyright © 1982 by Thomas Nelson. Used by permission. All rights reserved.

If you are interested in using the Mission Journal for your church or organization, email us for a complimentary starter kit: yourfriends@themissionjournal.com

TEAM

EDITOR
Louise Bierig

COVER DESIGN/TYPESETTING
Jay Park / JayPark.work

CREATOR
David Iskander / DavidIskander.com

GET IN TOUCH

SAY HELLO
yourfriends@themissionjournal.com

BE A STOCKIST/BULK ORDERS
sales@themissionjournal.com

TABLE OF CONTENTS
DEVOTIONAL GUIDE

PERSONAL STATEMENT   26

PREPARATION   35
1. Protection Against the Enemy *Ephesians 6:10-18*
2. Through Love Serve One Another *Galatians 5:13-15*
3. Rejoice in Him *Philippians 4:4-5*
4. He Knows You More Than You Do *Psalms 139*
5. The Lord's Law is Perfect *Psalms 19:7-10*
6. Love the Lord Your God *Deuteronomy 6:5*
7. Whatever is Right *Philippians 4:8*
8. Love One Another *1 John 3:11-15*
9. Cast All Your Anxieties on Him *1 Peter 5:7-9*
10. Joyful, Prayful, Thankful *1 Thessalonians 5:16-18*
11. Treasure in Heaven *Matthew 6:19-21*
12. Chosen *1 Peter 2:9-10*

IN COUNTRY   63
1. Thanksgiving and Prayer *Colossians 1:9-14*
2. Not of Fear *2 Timothy 1:7*
3. You are the Salt and the Light *Matthew 5:13-16*
4. Revelation of Jesus Christ *1 Peter 1:13-16*
5. Seek and Save the Lost *Luke 19:1-10*
6. The Willing Sufferer *Isaiah 53:1-12*
7. New Every Morning *Lamentations 3:22-24*
8. My Yoke is Easy *Matthew 11:28-30*
9. Faith has Healed You *Mark 5:25-34*
10. Run with Endurance *Hebrews 12:1-2*
11. Boast in the Lord *Psalm 34:1-3*
12. Help from the Spirit *Romans 8:26*
13. Fix your Eyes on the Unseen *2 Corinthians 4:18*
14. Do not be Anxious *Matthew 6:31-34*

WHEN YOU RETURN   95
1. Remember His Wondrous Works *Psalms 105:5*
2. Do Not Conform *Romans 12:1-2*
3. How Beautiful are the Feet *Isaiah 52:7*
4. The New has Come *2 Corinthians 5:17*
5. Content In Every Situations *Philippians 4:11-13*

PERSONAL COMMITMENTS   107

DEDICATION

To lifelong world changers and pioneers.
You're helping lives every day.

GOD ALWAYS SHOWS UP BIG

In Genesis 28 Jacob makes a commitment before he sets off for his calling:

"*If God stands by me and protects me on this journey on which I'm setting out, keeps me in food and clothing, and brings me back in one piece to my father's house, this God will be my God.*" Gen. 28:20 (MSG)

Don't you love Jacob's commitment and his pledge? Jacob is saying 'despite anything that could happen... despite fear, despite the unknown, and despite all the drama in my life right now, I will journey with You.'

Mission trips are a way we become like Jacob. We set out to trust God and obey His calling by heading on a faith adventure with Him!

And what does God do?

He shows up. And shows up BIG.

He gives us direction. He provides for us – be it finances, time, resources, donations, visas, passports, advice, training, time-off, ideas, or whatever is needed. And then, he brings us back, set out to never be the same again.

This journal provides a framework that becomes a testament of our God. It becomes a space where God shapes and shifts, speaks and directs, guides and instructs us on what's next. Exciting a bit?

Get ready! You are about to experience life-changing moments that keeps you charged back at home.

5 REASONS YOU WILL LOVE THE MISSION JOURNAL

A book of blank journal pages can pose an overwhelming commitment.

Our design house created a journal to help you easily stick to your commitment.

EASY TO USE
Ever sit down to journal after an amazing day, excited to document everything that happened, only to realize that you have 10 hours of writing and only 10 minutes of energy?

This journal is designed with that in mind--to give you the space and structure to simply engage with the story God is writing in your life during this season. Over time, you will become dependent on this journal--capturing what God has in store for you. All of it is formatted in a simple structure that works with you.

CONSTANT INSPIRATION
Motivation refreshes the spirit; but, motivation doesn't last. That is why quotes and verses applicable to your mission are touching every corner of this journal.

FOCUS
It's easy to miss all the good happening in our life by focusing our energy and effort on the negative. Each page of this journal is designed for you to emphasize the positive, no matter how tough it gets.

DIRECTION
Give order to the story God is crafting for your life. He gives you hints of love every day that convey purpose in your life. Why not capture these in an organized place? You may even find answers to major questions in your life as you look back and read in-between the lines.

A SENSE OF WINNING
If this is your first or tenth mission trip, you will have a running diary of what God is transforming in your journey. This will give you a sense of inspiration and remind you why you do what you do.

PHILOSOPHY OF THE MISSION JOURNAL

This journal combines three disciplines based on research, proven methods of growth, and understanding how God operates.

Specifically, we combine the discipline of missions, spiritual growth, and goal-setting to give you an all-in-one journal. Life changing experiences are only experiences until they produce life change.

MISSIONS
Never underestimate the power of missions. To dedicate 3 to 28 days to love and serve others is no small act. When we set out on such an effort, God makes His mark on our lives. This journal will give you room to record God's promises, fruit, testimonies, and love for you.

SPIRITUAL GROWTH
What makes this trip something God can use to transform people spiritually, including yourself? Between the morning and evening habits you create as you prepare for the trip, this journal will act as a wall plug to capture the still small voice encouraging you, building you, and transforming you.

GOAL SETTING
Writing our goals and commitments is one of the most prevailing behaviors for us to experience lasting change. After a mission trip, we come back with so much flexibility and realized potential. Built from tested and proven goal setting principles, the Mission Journal has been designed to help you beat complacency and experience real life change.

THE FIVE PART FRAMEWORK

Over and over again we found that mission trips require loads of different preparation.

Planning an orphan care or healing or evangelical missions trip requires diverse training.

Considering this, we realized there are spiritual markers that happen on nearly every trip.

Our 5-Part framework is the jolt of inspiration and structure you need to help you internalize fast-paced spiritual development to the fullest.

1st Spiritual Marker
Your Personal Statement

Understanding your why will keep you grounded when you set out on this journey. One thing is certain – you will face setbacks, feel spiritual attacks, and question your commitment to the trip. We outline the key questions that will give you the passion you need to push through difficult times. And, we write our commitment so we can return to the great decision we made when we said YES.

2nd Spiritual Marker
Preparation

Your mission trip is filled with meetings, planning, designing, writing your story, and gathering donations all while doing the most important task: growing spiritually. This journal is designed to give you room to identify your weekly tasks and jot down important notes from your meeting. While, most importantly, not overlooking the spiritual wins God is giving you along the way.

With two pages per week it's easy to handle and with one page per meeting, you will make sure to keep all the great inspiration for the long haul.

3rd Spiritual Marker
In Country

It's here. Your bags are packed, your passport in hand, and your spirit is ready. From here on out, God will show you his love and compassion in surprising ways. One day can be filled with 100 surprises. To give you room to capture it without feeling overwhelmed you complete your journal twice a day, for just a few moments each.

And since you collect more stories than you can write, we give you our method of quickly capturing the heart of a story without explanation.

4th Spiritual Marker
When You Return

Your journey may feel over, but it's not over yet. It's like God fed you a meal that could last a year. We breakdown a one-page weekly review for you to capture all the experiential knowledge and wisdom God poured out during the trip. When you look back in retrospect, you begin to understand things that you didn't in realtime speed.

5th Spiritual Marker
Personal Commitments

What is your return strategy? How do you take what you experienced and transfer it to the people back at home? Many people with great, world-changing ideas are not able to make them happen.

We designed this final section for you to first realign your heart with a gratitude map. From there, we outline and breakdown the joy of personal commitments, how to break bad habits, and how to step into your dreams. We define your next steps with an in-depth and well tested method of winning. Reentry doesn't have to be tough. We give you the tools and tricks to turn your experience with God into a lifestyle.

HOW TO USE THE MISSION JOURNAL

Our goal is to take those bursts of God's love that come at us each day as we prepare for our journey and document them. Our easy-to-follow structure and design allow you to document, review, and discover what God is doing in your life. Being able to connect the dots as we journey with God is one of the truest ways we know we have a relationship with him.

That way, when it comes time for you to take a step of faith, step outside your comfort zone, you won't dodge risk because of fear or complacency. You will be more open to faith adventures because you know that God will come through.

He is as big as He says He is and now you will have proof.

The ideal time to write in this journal is once a week as you prepare for the trip, before and after each team meeting, and every morning during your trip. The planner is designed to make the routine of journaling simple and painless.

WHEN TO WRITE IN THE MISSION JOURNAL

Returning to your journal will never be a chore. When updating your journal, you don't need to write 1000 words or spend more than 7 minutes with your journal at a time. We provide a framework that is simple and intutive for your trip so you can reach for your journal in the morning & evening each day.

The journal spans a 30-day timeframe.

The journal begins 12 days before your departure, includes 14 days in country, and continues 5 days upon your return.

PROMPTS FOR STUDY

We added these prompts for you as additional support

Slowly write out a verse & think about each word as you write it.

Write down your major impressions of the passage. What struck you from this passage?

How can you apply the observation so that it affects your life today?

Write out a prayer to God based on what you just learned and ask him to help you apply this truth in your life.

How does the theme apply to you personally?

Make a list of facts that you observe.

What does this passage teach about the Lord? Jesus? The Holy Spirit? Life? Yourself?

Is there a promise you can take for a situation you're facing?

LET'S

GET
STARTED!

PERSONAL STATEMENT

"Do all the good you can.
By all the means you can.
In all the ways you can.
In all the places you can.
At all the times you can.
To all the people you can.
As long as ever you can."
—John Wesley

UNDERSTANDING WHY
(18 minutes)

Understanding your personal why gives you a starting step to reveal what God is going to do on this trip. In this notebook, it doesn't matter what your why is.

All that matters is that you are honest.

Why is your trip important to God?
Write down what you know about God's heart, verses in scripture, and stories from the Bible that convey this point.

_____

_____

_____

Why are you going on this trip?

_____

_____

_____

Why do you believe this mission is important?

_____

_____

_____

QUESTIONS TO PONDER

What is one thing you would love to gain from this journey?
Maybe you want to deepen your relationship with God. Maybe you want to help make world a better place. Or, maybe you want to know God as your Provider/Shepherd/All-Powerful/Healer/Comforter/Helper/Hope/Faithful/Anchor/Father. Find what gets you excited about the journey.

_____

_____

What does God want to do spiritually within you?
Try and imagine what God is doing in your life right now and where he may be leading you. Jot down any thoughts that come to mind.

_____

_____

_____

> *Whenever you find yourself on the side of the majority, it is time to pause and reflect.*
>
> —*MARK TWAIN*

What fears do you have?
'What if something happens to me?,' 'I won't be useful,' or 'I have never done this before' are normal to experience when you commit to go. The best way to deal with them is to address them.

THOUGHT STARTERS
Fear of being judged, making mistakes, fear of missing out, fear of regret, fear of adjusting to the team/culture, fear of beingVunqualified, fear of travel/flying, fear of misguiding people spiritually, fear of bugs, fear of being alone, fear of the unknown, fear of germs, fear of being able to raise the money.

_____

_____

_____

Deepest Fears

Often, our greatest strength is on the other side of our deepest fear. It's time to have a one-on-one conversation with God. Use this section below to drop what the world expects of you, what society says you should be doing, and what those closest to you might say.

What are the barriers keeping you from chasing your dreams?

_____

_____

_____

"If you had never done anything that makes you nervous, where would you be right now?"

—MARCUS TAYLOR

DARE TO DREAM

Many barriers keep us from chasing our dreams. Most of them are false — ideas or conclusions we made up that are not real. It may make you nervous and give you the butterflies, dare to dream outside your comfort zone. As Bob Goff said it, "Comfortable people don't need Jesus."

For this upcoming trip, I want to be open to step outside my comfort zone regarding:

1. _____

2. _____

3. _____

THOUGHT STARTERS

Sharing your faith, cultural norms, public speaking, sharing the gospel, comforts in your home or work, your routine, germs, health, not having enough money for the future, your performance standard, seeing bugs, food standards, flying, talking to strangers.

TRIP COMMITMENT
(10 minutes)

It's time to clarify your commitment.
Below fill in everything you are committing to do on this mission trip. It can be as specific or broad as you like. No need to fret if details are still being planned. Just pray and ask God what three things you should commit to from today. Below is a template for you to fill out and then finalize on the next page.

Today is _____ (Date)

and I, _____ (Name),

am committing to go on a trip this _____ (Trip Date),

I desire to share God's love in _____ (Country).

In country I will...

1. _____

2. _____

3. _____

_____

THOUGHT STARTERS
Love the children at the orphanage, speak into young adults, build up the women, evangelize to three people groups, pray for the sick, allow God to help me step out my comfort zone.

TRIP COST $: _____

Now, write out your trip commitment on the following sheet in one paragraph.

TRIP COMMITMENT

DATE OF TRIP
_____

I desire to share God's love in…
_____
_____
_____
_____
_____
_____
_____
_____

TRIP COST
_____

SIGNATURE
_____

TODAY'S DATE
_____

"God is most glorified in us when we are most satisfied in Him."

—JOHN PIPER

PREPARATION

This is a season of life change.

We believe preparation is a game-changing component of your upcoming trip. You get out what you put in. Use this section to begin to ground yourself in the reality of spiritual formation in & around you.

The simplest thing you can do to start & end each day as you prepare, is make time to reflect about your trip. This simple format, includes a space for gratitude, a devotional, and a place to capture stories. The simple and intuitive design will refresh your heart anytime your nerves get the best of you.

Date:_____

PROTECTION AGAINST THE ENEMY

Ephesians 6:10-18

Morning

I'm grateful for...

_____

_____

_____

Prompt

A Spiritual battle is already underway because of the work you are about to do. How do you plan to prepare yourself?

_____

_____

_____

_____

_____

Most important tasks for today...

_____

_____

Any fears or anxieties?

_____

Preparation

"I am sending you."

—JESUS *(John 20:21)*

Stories / Notes

_____

_____

_____

Evening

List 3 amazing things (big or little) that happened

_____

_____

_____

On a scale of 1-10, how ready do you feel for your trip?

1   2   3   4   **5**   6   7   8   9   **10**

What are you looking forward to tomorrow?

_____

_____

_____

Date:_____

THROUGH LOVE SERVE ONE ANOTHER

Galatians 5:13-15

Morning

I'm grateful for...

_____

_____

_____

Prompt

As you prepare for your specific trip, what is one way you could serve others?

_____

_____

_____

_____

_____

Most important tasks for today...

_____

_____

Any fears or anxieties?

_____

Preparation

"God's part is to put forth power; our part is to put forth faith."

—ANDREW A. BONAR

Stories / Notes

_____

_____

_____

Evening

List 3 amazing things (big or little) that happened

_____

_____

_____

How ready do you feel for your trip?

1   2   3   4   5   6   7   8   9   10

What are you looking forward to tomorrow?

_____

_____

_____

Date:_____

REJOICE IN HIM

Philippians 4:4-5

Morning

I'm grateful for...

_____

_____

_____

Prompt

What does it mean to rejoice for you?

_____

_____

_____

_____

_____

Most important tasks for today...

_____

_____

Any fears or anxieties?

_____

Preparation

> *"Let my heart be broken with the things that break God's heart."*
>
> —BOB PIERCE

Stories / Notes

_____

_____

_____

Evening

List 3 amazing things (big or little) that happened

_____

_____

_____

How ready do you feel for your trip?

1 2 3 4 **5** 6 7 8 9 **10**

What are you looking forward to tomorrow?

_____

_____

_____

Date:_____

HE KNOWS YOU MORE THAN YOU DO

Psalm 139

Morning

I'm grateful for...

_____

_____

_____

Prompt

God knows you. He knew the journey you would take to get to this point,. What feels uncomfortable and out of place in this season?

_____

_____

_____

_____

_____

Most important tasks for today...

_____

_____

Any fears or anxieties?

_____

Preparation

> *"Our willingness to sacrifice for an enterprise is always in proportion to our faith in that enterprise."*
>
> —SAMUEL ZWUEMER

Stories / Notes

_____

_____

_____

Evening

List 3 amazing things (big or little) that happened

_____

_____

_____

How ready do you feel for your trip?

1   2   3   4   **5**   6   7   8   9   **10**

What are you looking forward to tomorrow?

_____

_____

_____

Date:_____

THE LORD'S LAW IS PERFECT

Psalm 19:7-10

Morning

I'm grateful for...

_____

_____

_____

Prompt

Write about three aspects of the Lord's law and what stands out?

_____

_____

_____

_____

_____

Most important tasks for today...

_____

_____

Any fears or anxieties?

_____

Preparation

> "*Worry does not empty tomorrow of its sorrows; it empties today of its strength.*"
>
> —CORRIE TEN BOOM

Stories / Notes

_____

_____

_____

Evening

List 3 amazing things (big or little) that happened

_____

_____

_____

How ready do you feel for your trip?

1   2   3   4   **5**   6   7   8   9   **10**

What are you looking forward to tomorrow?

_____

_____

_____

Date:_____

LOVE THE LORD YOUR GOD

Deuteronomy 6:5

Morning

I'm grateful for...

_____

_____

_____

Prompt

How does loving the Lord with all your heart, soul and might look like?

_____

_____

_____

_____

_____

_____

Most important tasks for today...

_____

_____

Any fears or anxieties?

_____

Preparation

"God isn't looking for people of great faith, but for individuals ready to follow him"

—HUDSON TAYLOR

Stories / Notes

_____

_____

_____

Evening

List 3 amazing things (big or little) that happened

_____

_____

_____

How ready do you feel for your trip?

1   2   3   4   5   6   7   8   9   10

What are you looking forward to tomorrow?

_____

_____

_____

Date:_____

WHATEVER IS RIGHT

Philippians 4:8

Morning

I'm grateful for...

_____

_____

_____

Prompt

Make a list of ways you can put this verse into practice.

_____

_____

_____

_____

_____

_____

Most important tasks for today...

_____

_____

Any fears or anxieties?

_____

Preparation

"He must increase, but I must decrese."

———JOHN THE BAPTIST

Stories / Notes

_____

_____

_____

Evening

List 3 amazing things (big or little) that happened

_____

_____

_____

How ready do you feel for your trip?

1   2   3   4   5   6   7   8   9   10

What are you looking forward to tomorrow?

_____

_____

_____

Date:_____

LOVE ONE ANOTHER

1 John 3:11-16

Morning

I'm grateful for...

_____

_____

_____

Prompt

What are some ways that you can love everyone; both your team members and those to whom you'll minister/serve?

_____

_____

_____

_____

_____

Most important tasks for today...

_____

_____

Any fears or anxieties?

_____

Preparation

> *"You have one business on earth—
> to save souls."*
>
> —JOHN WESLEY

Stories / Notes

_____

_____

_____

Evening

List 3 amazing things (big or little) that happened

_____

_____

_____

How ready do you feel for your trip?

1   2   3   4   **5**   6   7   8   9   **10**

What are you looking forward to tomorrow?

_____

_____

_____

Date:_____

CAST ALL YOUR ANXIETIES ON HIM

1 Peter 5:7-9

Morning

I'm grateful for...

_____

_____

_____

Prompt

As you approach your departure, what are you most anxious about concerning your trip?

_____

_____

_____

_____

_____

Most important tasks for today...

_____

_____

Any fears or anxieties?

_____

Preparation

> *"He is no fool who gives what he cannot keep to gain what he cannot lose."*
>
> —JIM ELLIOT

Stories / Notes

_____

_____

_____

Evening

List 3 amazing things (big or little) that happened

_____

_____

_____

How ready do you feel for your trip?

1　2　3　4　*5*　6　7　8　9　*10*

What are you looking forward to tomorrow?

_____

_____

_____

Date:_____

JOYFUL, PRAYFUL, THANKFUL

1 Thessalonians 5:16-18

Morning

I'm grateful for...

_____

_____

_____

Prompt

God's will for us is remarkable. What is one way you can incorporate this lifestyle into your daily routine?

_____

_____

_____

_____

_____

Most important tasks for today...

_____

_____

Any fears or anxieties?

_____

Preparation

"No reserves. No retreats. No regrets."

—WILLIAM BORDEN

Stories / Notes

_____

_____

_____

Evening

List 3 amazing things (big or little) that happened

_____

_____

_____

How ready do you feel for your trip?

1   2   3   4   5   6   7   8   9   10

What are you looking forward to tomorrow?

_____

_____

_____

Date:_____

TREASURE IN HEAVEN

Matthew 6:19-21

Morning

I'm grateful for...

_____

_____

_____

Prompt

Evaluate where you invest your resources. Does this help or hinder you growing closer to Jesus?

_____

_____

_____

_____

_____

Most important tasks for today...

_____

_____

Any fears or anxieties?

_____

Preparation

> *"The problems are worldwide, but the individual responses are eternally significant."*
>
> —— WORLD RELIEF

Stories / Notes

_____

_____

_____

Evening

List 3 amazing things (big or little) that happened

_____

_____

_____

How ready do you feel for your trip?

1   2   3   4   5   6   7   8   9   10

What are you looking forward to tomorrow?

_____

_____

_____

Date:_____

CHOSEN

1 Peter 2:9-10

Morning

I'm grateful for...

_____

_____

_____

Prompt

How does being chosen by God affect your value and worth?

_____

_____

_____

_____

_____

Most important tasks for today...

_____

_____

Any fears or anxieties?

_____

Preparation

"Jesus first calls us to himself, and then he calls us to exert serious effort to get his message out to the world."

—*JOHN RINEHART*

Stories / Notes

_____

_____

_____

Evening

List 3 amazing things (big or little) that happened

_____

_____

_____

How ready do you feel for your trip?

1   2   3   4   5   6   7   8   9   10

What are you looking forward to tomorrow?

_____

_____

_____

DEPARTURE TRAVEL NOTES

ITINERARY

Departure City

Arrival City

Transportation Info

NOTES/STORIES

DRAW OUT YOUR JOURNEY

"We have a God who delights in impossibilities"

—BILL SUNDAY

IN COUNTRY

Bags packed, passport in hand, and a heart full of excitement.

After hours of preparation and anticipation, today you set out on your journey.

Be open.

Be expectant.

Be ready.

It's time to free your mind of day-to-day stressors and make yourselves vulnerable to God's artisanship. The next step of your journey begins.

Day: _____   Date:_____

THANKSGIVING AND PRAYER

Colossians 1:9-14

Morning

I am grateful for...

_____

_____

_____

Prompt

People are praying for you as you embark on this adventure. Write down 3 people who helped you make this happen & pray for them.

_____

_____

_____

_____

_____

What are you most excited about today?

_____

_____

Any fears or anxieties?

_____

> *"My weakness is my greatest strength, for then I trust alone on Jesus, when I feel my own dependence."*
>
> —CHARLES SPURGEON

Story Capture

Capture today's best stories by writing down three components per story: who, where, and what made it special.

Example: (who) Michael and me with the kids, (where) in the dining hall, (what) reenacted the story of David & Goliath for the kids.

1. _____

2. _____

3. _____

Evening

One way you experienced God in a new way
_____

List one thing new—seen, met, eaten, touched, smelled, or experienced
_____

What are you looking forward to tomorrow?
_____

Day: _____   Date:_____

NOT OF FEAR

2 Timothy 1:7

Morning

I am grateful for...

_____

_____

_____

Prompt

What is your greatest fear right now? Share and talk to God.

_____

_____

_____

_____

_____

What are you most excited about today?

_____

_____

Any fears or anxieties?

_____

In Country

> *"Your job is not to leae a mark on earth, but a mark on hell."*
>
> —DAVID ISKANDER

Story Capture

Capture today's best stories by writing down three components per story: who, where, and what made it special.

1. _____

2. _____

3. _____

Evening

One way you experienced God in a new way

_____

List one thing new—seen, met, eaten, touched, smelled, or experienced

_____

What are you looking forward to tomorrow?

_____

Day: _____   Date:_____

YOU ARE THE SALT AND THE LIGHT

Matthew 5:13-16

Morning

I am grateful for...

_____

_____

_____

Prompt

What are some ways you can be a light to your team members and those you meet today?

_____

_____

_____

_____

_____

_____

What are you most excited about today?

_____

_____

Any fears or anxieties?

_____

> *"Passion, whatever a person is willing to suffer for."*
>
> —UNKNOWN

Story Capture

Capture today's best stories by writing down three components per story: who, where, and what made it special.

1. _____

2. _____

3. _____

Evening

One way you experienced God in a new way

_____

List one thing new—seen, met, eaten, touched, smelled, or experienced

_____

What are you looking forward to tomorrow?

_____

Day: _____   Date:_____

REVELATION OF JESUS CHRIST

1 Peter 1:13-16

Morning

I am grateful for...

_____

_____

_____

Prompt

In what areas of your life do you need to be reminded of your identity in Christ? How does this affect your actions and thoughts?

_____

_____

_____

_____

_____

_____

What are you most excited about today?

_____

_____

Any fears or anxieties?

_____

"For the son of man came to seek and save the lost."

—*JESUS* (Luke 19:10)

Story Capture

Capture today's best stories by writing down three components per story: who, where, and what made it special.

1. _____

2. _____

3. _____

Evening

One way you experienced God in a new way

_____

List one thing new—seen, met, eaten, touched, smelled, or experienced

_____

What are you looking forward to tomorrow?

_____

Day: _____   Date:_____

SEEK AND SAVE THE LOST

Luke 19:1-10

Morning

I am grateful for...

_____

_____

_____

Prompt

This is the kind of love Jesus has for everyone. How does this shape your view of Jesus? Like Zacchaeus, does it impact how you live?

_____

_____

_____

_____

_____

What are you most excited about today?

_____

_____

Any fears or anxieties?

_____

In Country

> *"Give thanks to God- he is good and his lover never quits."*
>
> —EZRA (1 Chronicles 16:34)

Story Capture

Capture today's best stories by writing down three components per story: who, where, and what made it special.

1. _____

2. _____

3. _____

Evening

One way you experienced God in a new way

_____

List one thing new—seen, met, eaten, touched, smelled, or experienced

_____

What are you looking forward to tomorrow?

_____

Day: _____   Date:_____

THE WILLING SUFFERER

Isaiah 53:1-12

Morning

I am grateful for...

_____
_____
_____

Prompt

Jesus willingly went to the cross because you are worth it to Him. What does it mean to you that Jesus willingly suffered for you? Spend time in prayer and reflection.

_____
_____
_____
_____
_____
_____

What are you most excited about today?

_____
_____

Any fears or anxieties?

_____

> *"Employ whatever God has entrusted you with, in doing good, all possible, good, in every possible kind & degree."*
>
> —JOHN WESLEY

Story Capture

Capture today's best stories by writing down three components per story: who, where, and what made it special.

1. _____

2. _____

3. _____

Evening

One way you experienced God in a new way

_____

List one thing new—seen, met, eaten, touched, smelled, or experienced

_____

What are you looking forward to tomorrow?

_____

Day: _____   Date:_____

NEW EVERY MORNING

Lamentations 3:22-24

Morning

I am grateful for...

_____

_____

_____

Prompt

God's faithfulness is always more than we can imagine. What does it mean to you when the Bible says, 'The Lord is my portion'?

_____

_____

_____

_____

_____

What are you most excited about today?

_____

_____

Any fears or anxieties?

_____

> *"Expect great things from God. Attempt great things for God."*
>
> —WILLIAM CAREY

Story Capture

Capture today's best stories by writing down three components per story: who, where, and what made it special.

1. _____

2. _____

3. _____

Evening

One way you experienced God in a new way

_____

List one thing new—seen, met, eaten, touched, smelled, or experienced

_____

What are you looking forward to tomorrow?

_____

Day: _____   Date:_____

MY YOKE IS EASY, & MY BURDEN IS LIGHT

Matthew 11:28-30

Morning

I am grateful for...

_____

_____

_____

Prompt

What heavy burdens do you need to give over to God? Pray for stamina and for His strength to finish strong.

_____

_____

_____

_____

_____

What are you most excited about today?

_____

_____

Any fears or anxieties?

_____

In Country

> *"Hope is found when needs are met."*
>
> —*UNKNOWN*

Story Capture

Capture today's best stories by writing down three components per story: who, where, and what made it special.

1. _____

2. _____

3. _____

Evening

One way you experienced God in a new way

_____

List one thing new—seen, met, eaten, touched, smelled, or experienced

_____

What are you looking forward to tomorrow?

_____

Day: _____   Date:_____

FAITH HAS HEALED YOU

Mark 5:25-34

Morning

I am grateful for...

_____

_____

_____

Prompt

Are you growing in your faith? In what ways has this trip challenged your faith?

_____

_____

_____

_____

_____

_____

What are you most excited about today?

_____

_____

Any fears or anxieties?

_____

"Fear not, I am the one who helps you."

—GOD *(Isaiah 41:13)*

Story Capture

Capture today's best stories by writing down three components per story: who, where, and what made it special.

1. _____

2. _____

3. _____

Evening

One way you experienced God in a new way

_____

List one thing new—seen, met, eaten, touched, smelled, or experienced

_____

What are you looking forward to tomorrow?

_____

Day: _____   Date:_____

RUN WITH ENDURANCE

Hebrews 12:1-2

Morning

I am grateful for...

_____

_____

_____

Prompt

There may be some hardships you have encountered or see around you. Describe what hardships you see.

_____

_____

_____

_____

_____

_____

What are you most excited about today?

_____

_____

Any fears or anxieties?

_____

> *"When you understand that life is a test, you realize that nothing is insignificant in your life."*
>
> —RICK WARREN

Story Capture

Capture today's best stories by writing down three components per story: who, where, and what made it special.

1. _____

2. _____

3. _____
   _____

Evening

One way you experienced God in a new way
_____

List one thing new—seen, met, eaten, touched, smelled, or experienced
_____

What are you looking forward to tomorrow?
_____

Day: _____ Date:_____

BOAST IN THE LORD

Psalm 34:1-3

Morning

I am grateful for...

_____

_____

_____

Prompt

When is it hardest to praise the Lord? Spend time in prayer this morning, praising God.

_____

_____

_____

_____

_____

_____

What are you most excited about today?

_____

_____

Any fears or anxieties?

_____

In Country

> *"He was rich, yet for your sake,
> he became poor."*
>
> —PAUL *(2 Corinthians 8:9)*

Story Capture

Capture today's best stories by writing down three components per story: who, where, and what made it special.

1. _____

2. _____

3. _____

Evening

One way you experienced God in a new way

_____

List one thing new—seen, met, eaten, touched, smelled, or experienced

_____

What are you looking forward to tomorrow?

_____

Day: _____   Date:_____

HELP FROM THE SPRIT

Romans 8:26

Morning

I am grateful for...

_____

_____

_____

Prompt

Take some time to wait on the Lord to speak to you in prayer. Praise God for helping us in our weakness.

_____

_____

_____

_____

_____

_____

What are you most excited about today?

_____

_____

Any fears or anxieties?

_____

In Country

> *"Lord Jesus, I am weary in your work, but not of it."*
>
> —GEORGE WHITEFIELD

Story Capture

Capture today's best stories by writing down three components per story: who, where, and what made it special.

1. _____

2. _____

3. _____

Evening

One way you experienced God in a new way

_____

List one thing new—seen, met, eaten, touched, smelled, or experienced

_____

What are you looking forward to tomorrow?

_____

Day: _____   Date:_____

FIX YOUR EYES ON THE UNSEEN

2 Corinthians 4:18

Morning

I am grateful for...

_____

_____

_____

Prompt

How can you be more in-tune with the things unseen? Pray for the things going on in the spiritual realm that are happening because of your ministry.

_____

_____

_____

_____

_____

What are you most excited about today?

_____

_____

Any fears or anxieties?

_____

In Country

> "Declare his glory among the nations,
> his marvelous deeds among all peoples."
>
> —EZRA *(1 Chronicles 16:24)*

Story Capture

Capture today's best stories by writing down three components per story: who, where, and what made it special.

1. _____

2. _____

3. _____

Evening

One way you experienced God in a new way

_____

List one thing new—seen, met, eaten, touched, smelled, or experienced

_____

What are you looking forward to tomorrow?

_____

Day: _____   Date:_____

DO NOT BE ANXIOUS

Matthew 6:31-34

Morning

I am grateful for...

_____

_____

_____

Prompt

Write down the anxieties that you're feeling about heading home. As you prepare for the journey home, pray and release them to God.

_____

_____

_____

_____

_____

What are you most excited about today?

_____

_____

Any fears or anxieties?

_____

> *"My one design is to bring poor souls to Jesus Christ."*
>
> —GEORGE WHITEFIELD

Story Capture

Capture today's best stories by writing down three components per story: who, where, and what made it special.

1. _____

2. _____

3. _____

Evening

One way you experienced God in a new way

_____

List one thing new—seen, met, eaten, touched, smelled, or experienced

_____

What are you looking forward to tomorrow?

_____

DEPARTURE TRAVEL NOTES

ITINERARY

Departure City

Arrival City

Transportation Info

NOTES/STORIES

DRAW OUT YOUR JOURNEY

"You can't connect the dots looking forward; you can only connect them looking backwards... believing that the dots will connect down the road will give you the confidence to follow your heart even when it leads you off the well worn path."

—STEVE JOBS

WHEN YOU RETURN

After the trip, there are mixed emotions and feelings.

While we share all the amazing stories with family and friends, we must also confront our fears and pain points that keep us from chasing our God-given dreams back at home. Sharing our story isn't about the art of storytelling. It's about embracing the emotions of telling our story. The first five days upon your return are the most critical. Settling back into your old routine of life is normal. What's not normal is to come back, settle into your schedule, and not grow from your experience.

This final section will help you process your trip so you can capture valuable takeaways from this experience. The journal is designed to give you room to revisit everything. The potential you unlocked in country could send you charging into your next adventure.

Date:_____

REMEMBER HIS WONDROUS WORKS

Psalm 105:5

Morning

I'm grateful for...

_____

_____

_____

Prompt

What are the first things that come to mind when you look back on your trip experience?

_____

_____

_____

_____

_____

_____

_____

_____

_____

_____

> *"The Bible tells us that God cares less about how much we have and more about what we do with it."*
>
> —JOHN RINEHART

Evening

Prayer

Thank God for some of the great things God did. Be ready to share them with family and friends.

_____

_____

_____

_____

_____

_____

_____

Question

What is difficult to cope with after the trip?

_____

_____

Date:_____

DO NOT CONFORM

Romans 12:1-2

Morning

I'm grateful for...

_____

_____

_____

Prompt

What new ways of thinking have come from this experience? Is there anything you learned that you never knew before?

_____

_____

_____

_____

_____

_____

_____

_____

_____

> "One act of obedience is better than one hundred sermons."
>
> —DIETRICH BONHOEFFER

Evening

Prayer

Ask God seals this experience within your heart and mind.

_____

_____

_____

_____

_____

_____

Question

How is your view of God changing because of this experience?

_____

_____

Date:_____

HOW BEAUTIFUL ARE THE FEET

Isaiah 52:7

Morning

I'm grateful for...

_____

_____

_____

Prompt

What does this verse mean to you?

_____

_____

_____

_____

_____

_____

_____

_____

_____

When You Return

> *"Surely the Lord is in this place,
> and I did not know it"*
>
> —JACOB *(Genesis 28:16)*

Evening

Prayer

Thank God for choosing you to be apart of this mission.

_____

_____

_____

_____

_____

_____

_____

Question

What has improved since the trip, big or little?

_____

_____

Date:_____

THE OLD HAS GONE, THE NEW HAS COME

2 Corinthians 5:17

Morning

I'm grateful for...

_____

_____

_____

Prompt

What 'old' has passed away in your life? Are there any new mindsets you have adopted from your experience?

_____

_____

_____

_____

_____

_____

_____

_____

_____

"I love to live on the brink of eternity."
—DAVID BRAINERD

Evening

Prayer

*Pray for those who accepted Christ during your trip.
Pray for those you encountered on your trip.*

_____

_____

_____

_____

_____

_____

_____

Question

What is one conversation that keeps coming up again and again this week?

_____

_____

Date:_____

CONTENT IN EVERY SITUATION

Philippians 4:11-13

Morning

I'm grateful for...

_____

_____

_____

Prompt

What does it mean to be content in every situation? What is one way you can be content in your day-to-day back home?

_____

_____

_____

_____

_____

_____

_____

_____

_____

When You Return

> *"The Son of Man came not to be served but to serve."*
>
> —*JESUS* (Matthew 20:28a)

Evening

Prayer

Ask God to help you be content in the easy and difficult times..

_____

_____

_____

_____

_____

_____

Question

What has God been saying to you in your quiet time?

_____

_____

"To achieve exceptional things, you must hold yourself to exceptional standards, regardless of what others may think."

—ADAM BRAUN

PERSONAL COMMITMENT

This part of the journey is challenging and exciting. God is speaking, and now is our time to listen.

How is your life going to change after this radical experience? Better yet, how will the world be better off thanks to you having been on this earth?

Start by setting two goals: one personal goal and one professional goal. If you are a student, instead of setting a professional goal, create an educational goal.

Studies by Yale and Harvard have shown that writing down goals increases the likelihood of accomplishing them. At Harvard, researchers asked an MBA class upon graduation:

Do you have specific goals for the future with a concrete plan for their attainment? Only 3 percent answered yes, while the majority of the other students, about 84 percent, had no goals at all.

The 3 percent that set goals went on to make 10 times as much as the 97 percent. Imagine having 10 times more impact for the Kingdom by simply spending a few minutes writing your goals. Let's begin.

GRATITUDE MAP

Gratitude reveals our hope and reminds us that when you feel gratitude, love, playfulness, ease, creativity, growth, appreciation, joy, and drive, you're at your best. Use this gratitude map to recount the countless positive moments you have experienced during this season. Show your gratefulness to people, things, stories, and conversations that transformed your life.

Three amazing people you met during the trip

_____

_____

_____

Three amazing people on your team

_____

_____

_____

Great gifts of knowledge and experience you have been given

_____

_____

_____

Ways you unlocked more potential from yourself during this trip

_____

_____

_____

Great things you learned about culture and people

_____

_____

_____

> *"If we have a right view of ourselves in this world as pilgrims, as children of God going to our Father, everything falls into its true perspective."*
>
> —MARTYN LLOYD-JONES

HOW TO SUCCESSFULLY SET GOALS

5 PARTS OF A GOAL

ACTIONABLE
Make the goal specific. Set goals that can be accomplished. That means, give them a measurement. For example, spend 30 minutes with God every day. The key is 30 minutes. It's measureable. Anything else could be subjective.

TIME BOUND
Goals mean nothing if they don't expire. Parkinson's law says that, "work expands so as to fill the time available for its completion." In other words, the amount of time you give yourself to complete your goal is likely the time it will take you to finish it. If you don't set an end date, chances are the goal will not be a priority. Set your goals to end by a particular time or date.

MEANINGFUL
This is the why in goal setting. The goal must be important enough for you to do whatever it takes to achieve it. Ultimately, it must be your goal, not a goal that sounds good. Find what you have always wanted to achieve and go after it. Your goal has to be something that makes you come alive so you can put your dreams into action!

HOW
Identify the daily/weekly/monthly actionable habits, disciplines, or behaviors necessary to achieve your goal. Setting a goal is like putting a mile marker in front of you and then tracing back your steps to how you will get there.

MEANS
Who will you need help from to achieve your goal? Or, what will you need to achieve this goal? Who may be friends, small groups, or mentors? What may be a specific app, tool, or new schedule should you adapt to pursue your goal?

YOUR MOST AMBITIOUS GOAL

Before writing your goal and considering all the factors of real life, take a moment and pause. Turn off your rational brain and dream.

We tend to overestimate what we could do in a year and underestimate what we could do in ten years. Think ahead and dream big.

This could be the start of transforming big dreams into reality. Talk to God and answer this question:

What is your most ambitious goal?

_____

_____

Below, let's write out our personal and professional goals.

PERSONAL GOAL

THOUGHT STARTERS
Volunteer at church, join a spiritual group, read more books on spirituality, learn a language, time freedoms, identify who you want to meet, meet your ideal weight, increase stamina, increase amount of charitable giving, reduce cholesterol count, reduce caffeine, run a marathon, spend more time with family, visit relatives once a month, dedicate evenings to children, plan a date night with spouse every week.

I want to accomplish _____
(specific/measurable)

By _____
(date)

Because _____
(3 reasons/benefits/reasons not to give up)

_____

_____

I'll need to _____
(daily/weekly/monthly habits, disciplines, or behaviors you need to accomplish this goal)

With _____
(who or what will you need help from?)

PROFESSIONAL/EDUCATIONAL GOAL

THOUGHT STARTERS
Increase income, increase savings, begin investing, become debt free, start/finish major projects, increase customer satisfaction, learn new skills, get a promotion, find a mentor, read 30 minutes every day, take a course, join a supportive organization, hire a coach, mentor someone else, complete classes, graduate from college, complete an online program.

I want to accomplish _____
(specific/measurable)

By _____
(date)

Because _____
(3 reasons/benefits/reasons not to give up)

_____

_____

I'll need to _____
(daily/weekly/monthly habits, disciplines, or behaviors you need to accomplish this goal)

With _____
(who or what will you need help from?)

Once you finalize your goals, make sure they are written, prominently displayed and regularly reviewed.

"Discipline is just choosing between what you want now and what you want most."

—DALE PARTRIDGE

PERSONAL GOAL

_____
_____
_____
_____
_____

PROFESSIONAL GOAL

_____
_____
_____
_____
_____

CHOOSE WHAT TO LEAVE OUT

HEDONIC TREADMILL

Definition: A theory proposing that people stay at about the same level of happiness regardless of what happens to them.

More simply put, an example of the Hedonic Treadmill is when we pray, receive amazing blessing from God, yet still feel the same as before. We realize the thing we predicated our happiness on has came to pass but our happiness hasn't changed.

Imagine this playing out when life gets better, but we still live in a rut, draw the same negative conclusions, and sabotage our success. The underlying theme here: Regardless of income, good health, and our relationships, we want more. Our happiness doesn't seem to improve as our possessions, position, and power do.

Most people have a few things they do that cause the majority of their pain (like binge eat, staying up late watching TV/Netflix, or not having a budget). Instead of living this cycle year after year, you can change the same underlying tendency by simply realizing what they are. A great question that Tim Ferriss, NY Times Bestselling author, puts forth is,

What 20% of activities are causing 80% of your negative emotions?

IDENTIFY

What is the single greatest timewaster in your life?

_____

What is the next biggest timewaster in your life?

_____

STOP DOING LIST

Good leaders have clear to-do list. Great leaders have a 'stop doing' list. What we commit to stop doing can be just as or more important than what we start doing. A Stop doing list always heightens your focus with your passion, purpose, and calling. What is costing your time, energy, and resources that does not fit?

List three things you should stop doing

THOUGHT STARTERS
Drinking caffeine, watching Netflix, eating out, working during family time, trying to please others, hanging out with…, eating late, spending time on Facebook.

_____

_____

_____

WHAT'S SHAPING YOU?

Maybe you have heard this quote from Charlie Tremendous Jones before, "*You are the same person you are today in five years' time, except for two things: The books you read and the company you keep.*"

Our associations unconsciously guide our future. Here, take a few moments to intentionally reshape your future in the direction you want. Ponder, dream, imagine, and clarify.

MENTORSHIP
Consider committing to a coach, trainer, or a spiritual guide to reinforce your growth. Mentors are not just in person, they can come via books, seminars, online videos, and online programs.

_____

_____

_____

EXPANDED ASSOCIATION
With your goals in mind, who do you need to be around more often?

_____

_____

_____

LIMITED ASSOCIATION
Are there people you may need to pull back from a bit? Your season of life may be different than theirs. They are good people, but not necessarily going where you are going, have the same ambition, or desire the same lifestyle.

_____

_____

_____

DISASSOCIATION
Sometimes the first step in achieving your dream is breaking off what is keeping you from your dream. There are people who draw negative emotions in you—they gossip, complain, blame, and never seem to be moving forward. They constantly take mental and emotional energy from you, rather than filling you up. This could also be negative, fear mongering, and empty sitcoms via TV, YouTube, social media, websites, or magazines.

_____

_____

_____

BOOKS
What books can you read that will help you step closer to your goals? What books will help you stay inspired, positive, and spiritually fed?

_____

_____

_____

MISSION TRIP MIRACLE CHECKLIST

This is the final round-up. Use this section below and update it throughout your journey.

Did God open the time needed from work or school to go?

YES/NO

Did God raise all the funds for the trip?

YES/NO

Three people you are thankful supported you in prayer or financially

_____

_____

_____

Three people you are thankful for during this season

_____

_____

_____

"I will not leave you until I have done what I have promised you."

—GOD *(Genesis 28:15)*

One thing you discovered about God
_____

One thing you discovered about people
_____

One thing you discovered about yourself
_____

One blessing God used to show you His love preparing for the trip
_____

One blessing God used to show you His love during the trip
_____

One blessing God used to show you His love after the trip
_____

TRAVEL GOALS

Mark an X on every city, state, region, or continent you want to visit.

TAKE-AWAYS

What one fear did you overcome during this experience?

_____

Your top 3 takeaways from the trip

_____

_____

_____

What single thing would you like to make absolutely certain you do (if at all possible) during your lifetime?

_____

A FINAL CHECKPOINT

CONGRATULATIONS!

You've just finished 30 days of spiritual growth! That must feel amazing, admit it. We are so thrilled to see you journey through such an amazing opportunity.

We ask just one small favor: email us your experience with the journal yourfriends@themissionjournal.com

IF YOU ENJOYED THIS, PLEASE SHARE IT WITH FRIENDS.

If you are interested in using the Mission Journal for your church, organization, or agency, email us and we will mail you our complimentary starter kit: yourfriends@themissionjournal.com

The Standards of Excellence (SOE) in Short-Term Mission is an accrediting and resourcing body for those who send, receive, facilitate and support short-term mission (STM) endeavors.

The Mission Journal is in partnership with the Standards of Excellence in Short-Term Mission to give users the ultimate mission's experience.

LEARN MORE AT SOE.ORG

TRAVEL NOTES

ITINERARY

Arrival Date & Time

Airline/Flight/Train/Bus Info

Departure City

Arrival City

IN COUNTRY CONTACT

Name of Host

Host Phone

Host Email

Place of Stay Name

Place of Stay Address

ADDITIONAL NOTES

TRAVEL TIP
Take a photo of your passport, visa, and ticket so you can have that information on your device upon arrival. It's good to have a pen handy, too

Made in the USA
Columbia, SC
07 September 2019